STOP CHASING TWO RABBITS

IS BUSINESS OWNERSHIP RIGHT FOR YOU?

PAT HYLAND

Stop Chasing Two Rabbits

Is Business Ownership Right for You?

Copyright © 2024 by Pat Hyland

Published by Book Ripple
www.BookRipple.com

All rights reserved. No part of this book may be reproduced or transmitted in any form or by any means, electronic or mechanical, including photocopying and recording, or by an information storage and retrieval system, without permission in writing from the author.

ISBN: 978-1-951797-83-6
Printed in the United States of America

To contact the author, go to:
www.StopChasingTwoRabbits.com

Chasing one rabbit is hard enough,
let alone trying to chase two.

Dedication

What Matters Most

I dedicate this book to what matters most ... the people in my life.

First and foremost, this means my wife Cindy for her unconditional support and steadfast love for our family. I've never known anyone who personally sacrifices so much that others will be blessed. Thank you for always believing in me and being my biggest cheerleader.

To our daughter, Chelsi, and her husband, Sam, who have blessed us with our two beautiful grandchildren, Maddox, and Juliet. To our son, Blake, who is already the man I hope to become one day. I've never known anyone who uses his faith and positive view of life to bless so many people each day. To my mom, for all the sacrifices you made for us kids so that we would be able to pursue our own passions.

Also, I'm incredibly grateful for the quality people whom I have had the opportunity to work with over the years, including Robert Tunmire, who challenged Cindy and me to start our own journey toward financial independence. To Mike Hawkins who provided me with so much inspiration within this book and by showing me how to positively challenge and coach aspiring entrepreneurs in taking their next steps toward business ownership. To Bill Moyer who has spent well over a decade mentoring me in all aspects of my life. To Brandon Haire who has taught me what true servant leadership looks like and how Christ can still be a part of today's workplace.

Finally, to those on my teams over the years who have encouraged me to write this book including John Dobelbower, Tyler Burnett, and Aaron Rosen.

Preface

Where It All Begins

Are you considering owning your own business? If you dream of business ownership, the goal of this book is to help you define your dreams and goals in such a way that you will have an untethered resolve to do what's necessary to make your dreams come true.

But I also have a word of caution as there is a possibility that this book may help you determine that business ownership may not be right for you. The good news is that the answer of what is best for "you" lies within the subsequent chapters of this book.

Confucius said, "The man who chases two rabbits, catches neither." The two rabbits we are going to focus on in this book are whether you need to pursue business ownership to achieve your personal and financial goals, or whether you should continue with your current job or career path.

To say it another way:

> Do you need to keep doing what you've been doing, or do you need to make a change?

Over the last 30 plus years, I had the opportunity to coach thousands of individuals on which path they should take. Even though each journey was different, the ones who ended up achieving their goals to the fullest were the ones who first took their time to clearly define which path was best for them, and then they acted on it.

The ones who didn't achieve their goals often tried to chase both paths (rabbits) at the same time and never fully achieved either. Confucius is spot on!

For me, I have always been entrepreneurial in my thinking. The same with Cindy, my wife. And we have worked hard as it was ingrained into us by our parents.

After we were married, I worked full-time and she took the lead in helping start new businesses on the side. We did everything together and learned a lot every step of the way.

What really changed everything for us was when Robert Tunmire, a successful businessman and philanthropist, asked if we were working toward financial independence.

We said we were.

Then he asked if we had a written, specific definition of what our financial independence looked like, when we were going to get there, and how we were going to get there.

We said, "Uh, no."

He pressed us further, asking us what the likelihood was that we would arrive somewhere when we didn't know when we would get there, how we were going to get there, and what it would look like when we got there?

We admitted, "It's not likely at all."

He then asked us a practical question about how we would go about planning a family vacation someplace stateside or overseas.

We explained that we would first figure out where we wanted to go, then work out the necessary steps like booking airline tickets, car rental, hotels, and the specific sights or attractions that we wanted to see.

He smiled, and we knew what was coming. He noted that the process towards achieving financial independence and going on a family vacation was much the same.

Robert then gave us some time to collectively write down our definition of financial independence. This exercise wasn't as easy as we would have thought, and after 10 minutes, all Cindy and I had written down was:

- being debt free
- having our home paid off (being our biggest asset at the time)

- having saved enough money so we could retire comfortably

We shared with Robert our definition for financial independence. He listened, and then explained that being debt free was not the goal but rather a part of doing what we needed to do to get financially independent.

Tongue in cheek, he said that he knew a lot of homeless people who were debt free but were not financially independent. He also noted that the value of our home should not be included in our goal because it wasn't income producing, whereas rental homes or commercial real estate could be assets.

So with the help from Robert, we formulated our own definition of financial independence. This is what we came up with:

> By the age of 55, we will have a minimum of $5,000,000 of income-producing assets generating a minimum of 5% return, which will provide us $250,000 a year of passive income without working and no real personal debt.

This exercise was extremely helpful because we, Cindy and I together, finally had our goals clearly defined. We had a compass to gauge every financial, career, and personal decision.

Up until then we didn't know if the decisions were taking us toward or away from our goals.

Once we clarified our goals, we had clarity on the future decisions we would make for us and for our family.

Don't get me wrong, we haven't always made the right choices along the way. At the age of 46, and after working on our plan for 17 years, we were less than halfway to our goal.

Then the unexpected happened, and it changed everything.

"The older I get, the more I see a straight path where I want to go. If you're going to hunt for elephants, don't get off the trail for a bunny."
– T. Boone Pickens

Contents

DEDICATION: What Matters Most	4
PREFACE: Where It All Begins	6
CHAPTER ONE: Are You on Track?	14
CHAPTER TWO: Forced to Change	18
CHAPTER THREE: Box #1 – Your Dreams and Goals	34
CHAPTER FOUR: Box #2 – The Fork in the Road	48
CHAPTER FIVE: Box #3 – The "How" to Your "Why"	58
CHAPTER SIX: Box #4 – The Mirror	76
CHAPTER SEVEN: Your Definition	86
CONCLUSION: Always Adjust	90

"Achieved by dauntless resolution
and unconquerable faith."
– On the Wright Brothers National Memorial
Historical Marker (hmdb.org)

CHAPTER ONE
Are You on Track?

There is one question that can *impact* your life right now ... and if you keep asking yourself this question, it will *change* your life!

Here it is.

With all honesty, ask yourself:

> "Am I on track to meet my dreams and goals, needs, and quality of life requirements, or do I need to do something different to achieve them?"

Follow that question with this one:

> "If things continue over the next few years as they have over the past few years, without making any real significant changes, will I be on track to accomplish all of the goals that are important to me and my family?"

Personal, family and even career circumstances can change, and they can change in the blink of an eye! So, you should ask yourself these questions often as they will help keep you on track to achieve what's most important to you.

In so doing, you will be able to reflect on all you have accomplished. You can celebrate the wins you've had along the way with fresh zeal and passion!

Are you on track? Are you going to keep going down the path you are on, or do you need to do something different?

Your answer will help determine what you will do next.

Unfortunately, most people go through life thinking they have plenty of time to make the changes that will help them accomplish their goals. But every day more of that time slips away.

I remember another lesson that Robert shared with Cindy and me about time. He said that a lot of people believe they "have time" to do this or that, when in all actuality time is not something we "have" but only something we "lose" every single day. When it's gone, it's gone forever.

Because people fail to take action in the present, always thinking they will address it in the future, they naturally end up never achieving the goals that they had for themselves and their families.

It isn't just running out of time that affects people, they lack a clear understanding of what their goals actually are. And if they don't know where they are going, how are they going to get there?

Your goals need to be in front of you at all times, and you need to review them often, if not daily.

Why? Because the awareness of your goals will affect your decisions, plans, and steps you take on a daily basis.

And if the current path you are on is not working, then being aware of that fact is vital to your success. Don't wait a year or two (or a lifetime!) to change directions. Get back on track now!

Yes, it can be scary to make changes, but those who change course are always more likely to hit their targets than those who refuse to make the necessary changes.

Asking yourself these tough questions does take guts. It really does. That's why very few people do it.

I remember coaching Mark, a 50-year-old businessman, who "suddenly" realized he was running out of time. His kids were all out of the house, he had a stable job, and $230,000 in his 401k, but he was a long way away from being able to retire.

He and his wife had "hoped" for many things but had never worked out a plan. The good news was that Mark was doing something about his financial goals, but the bad news was that he had a lot less time to do it in!

Are you on target to reach your goals?

This applies to not just your career but also your health, diet, spiritual walk, relationships, home, mind, family, and more.

Are you on track?

Chapter Two

Forced to Change

Sometimes, it takes a defining moment to bring clarity to your situation and hold up a mirror to yourself in pursuit of your dreams and goals.

When our son, Blake, was 14 years old, he competed at a very high level in gymnastics. In fact, he had been in competition since he was 6 years old. He loved showing off his acrobatic skills and learning new routines.

He lived in the gym!

However, our world changed dramatically when Blake had a gymnastic accident.

On that fateful day at the gym, he was learning a new maneuver for his floor routine by tumbling into a foam pit. He was one of the oldest, and the many younger kids were using the wide side of the vaulting area that led into the foam pit.

Blake's 50-foot tumble tramp was set up in front of a high-bar pit that was only seven feet wide. That's pretty narrow in comparison to the much wider regular foam pits.

On one of his first attempts, Blake came full speed down the tumble tramp. When he vaulted, he overcompensated and came off cockeyed. As he was flying through the air and preparing for his landing, his waist hit the side of the foam pit and his head whipped down into the exposed concrete! A lady standing next to the pit said it sounded like a bowling ball hitting concrete after falling from a 10-story building.

He then slid back into the foam pit, which seemed to swallow him alive. They called 911 and an ambulance arrived about 10 minutes later.

At this time, Blake was being supported in the foam pit by his coach. I'll never forget the gurgling sounds that my son was making.

The EMTs secured Blake to a board and rushed him to the local hospital where they immediately did a CAT-scan. Those images went to the on-call neurosurgeon who immediately rushed to the hospital.

When he arrived, he told us that Blake needed an emergency craniotomy and removed the right side of his skull. Blake had hit his head so hard that the blood vessels in his brain burst and blood was quickly filling up his brain cavity. The resulting increased pressure would kill Blake if they didn't do something soon.

The doctor explained that they didn't usually perform craniotomies at that hospital on children younger than 18. Instead, they would life-flight the patient to a hospital in the Dallas-Fort Worth area or down to Temple, but Blake's condition was so bad that he feared Blake would probably die on the flight.

He asked our permission to perform the surgery, and in a daze, we gave it.

Our heads were spinning. Our whole world had instantly changed.

Blake was quickly fading on the operating table, but they were able to successfully remove his bone flap (the right side of his skull about the size of a small nerf football). Then they prepped him for a flight to Cook Children's Hospital in Fort Worth.

The doctor came out of the operating room and asked us a crazy question, "What would you like to do with Blake's bone flap?"

We didn't know what to say.

He explained that one day, hopefully, Blake could have the bone flap reattached after his brain swelling had subsided.

We had two options: have the doctors make an incision in Blake's abdomen and put the bone flap in there for safe keeping (the body would provide the bone with the nutrients it needed until it was time to put it back on) or pack the bone flap on ice until it was time to put back on.

We chose the second option. It seemed like an additional cut to Blake's body would not be helpful.

Blake was then life-flighted to Cook Children's Hospital in Fort Worth. We were about to jump in our car and make the two-hour drive to the hospital when someone wisely told us to first go home and pack our bags full of clothes. They said we would probably be there for a while, and they were right.

Our daughter Chelsi (who lived in the Fort Worth area) was already there at the hospital with Blake by the time Cindy and I arrived.

At one point Blake's body temperature went up to 106 degrees and they wrapped him in a cooling system to try to keep his temperature down. Because the brain regulates body temperature, this temperature increase was not surprising, but Blake's temperature was continuing to rise which became a major concern.

As the five nurses and doctors surrounded Blake's bed and worked to keep his temperature down, I asked the ER physician what Blake's chances of survival were to make it through the day.

"About 50/50 at best," he stated.

At this time, I gathered my wife, family, and close friends in the courtyard of the hospital, and we prayed. I thanked our amazing God for giving us Blake. I shared how ever since Blake was a baby that we always told Blake that we were so blessed to be his parents, but that God was his Father as well. We told God that we truly wanted Him to save Blake, but that Blake was His first and that we would love Him and honor Him either way. We asked for a miracle to save Blake's life and give us our son back.

Within an hour, Blake's body temperature came back to a manageable 101 degrees!

Five days after the accident, Cindy and I were asked to meet with several doctors, nurses, clergy, and hospital administration. It felt ominous.

We had almost lost Blake three times in the first five days since the accident, as his brain had swelled up and out of his skull.

When we got in the meeting room, all of Blake's most recent MRI images were on the monitors throughout the room. They explained that a healthy brain looks grey on the images and that white shows areas that are dead.

All of Blake's right temporal lobe was white, his frontal lobe was all white, and because his head hit the concrete so hard that his brain shook in his skull, a strip on the left side of his brain was white as well. Dead and gone.

They also explained that if Blake did live that he would most likely be on a ventilator in a nursing home for the rest of his life.

We were both crying and overwhelmed at that point, but I was able to momentarily compose myself and share with everyone in the room that Cindy and I believe our God not only died for our sins on the cross, but that He was also a God of healing and that our son would walk out of that hospital one day.

One of the doctors replied, "We hope you prove us wrong."

It was then and there that we put a stake in the ground by claiming God's promises of healing, and over time we and many others would see His love, grace, and compassion at work.

Blake was in a coma for almost seven weeks. During that time, he lost weight (from over 140 pounds to a mere 110 pounds), was in a diaper, and laid immobile in bed with his eyes fixated to the right (toward his brain injury). He also couldn't talk, had an external feeding tube ported in his stomach, and had a trachea to breathe through. What's more, the hospital wanted to send us home.

We wouldn't allow it! I had contacted the best traumatic brain injury doctors in the country, and they had explained that the very best thing to do was to get a minimum of one year of intensive therapy as this would get Blake to at least 80% of his full capability, then work on improving the remaining 20% over the coming years.

But sending Blake home early, the doctors said, would limit Blake to just 40% of his capability long-term.

We stayed and put a sign above Blake's hospital bed that read, "Full Restoration In Process."

Hours and hours of therapy and treatment went on and on, and we documented every little victory Blake had, from the first time he spoke, to the first time he took his first step, and to the first time he ate food on his own. There were dozens of small victories that we celebrated along the way.

Three months later, Blake walked out of that hospital! While this milestone was an incredible victory, it was also the start of Blake's continued journey to recovery. Cindy quit her job and for 16 months she and Blake stayed at the Ronald McDonald House in Dallas so Blake could go to Neuro-rehab from 9-4 every day.

It wasn't long into Blake's recovery that Cindy and I began to ask ourselves, "Who will take care of Blake if something happens to us?"

We knew we didn't want Blake to go to a state institution. We wanted him to be cared for at a higher level. How would he cope if something happened to us? We found a company that does life plans studies, and three weeks later they shared with us that it would cost no less than 12 million dollars and up to 23 million to care for Blake to the level we wanted.

We hadn't figured that into our financial goals!

Prior to Blake's accident, we were not quite halfway to our original goal of five million, much less 12-23 million.

I went back to work and was in a complete mental fog, trying to adjust to our "new normal." I was shell shocked, sitting in front of my computer, trying to determine how to get back to my day-to-day job and the responsibilities that came along with it.

Frankly, my heart, mind, and soul weren't in my work. How could they be? They were with my son and my wife.

We were being forced to change, but for lasting change to really take place, it must come from a personal choice.

Were we really, truly willing to change?

Did we want it badly enough?

If so, it had to be our choice.

As I stared blankly at my computer screen, I looked down to the bottom of my monitor and saw a quote that I had taped to it many years before. I had read this quote hundreds of times before, but it never hit home until that day. It says:

> "If you will do what most will not do for just the next few years, then you can do what they cannot do for the rest of your life." – Wade Cook

I thought, "What if this is true?! What if Cindy and I went ALL in for just the next few years." Right then, I knew what I needed to do, and that was make a change! I knew change was essential, as we had that 12-23-million-dollar number firmly hanging over our heads.

But I also knew that going all in meant getting Cindy on board as well, or achieving our new goals would be much harder, if not impossible.

I immediately called Cindy and read her the same quote. Then I asked her, "Are you in?"

Cindy without hesitation said "absolutely" and at that time we made the commitment to do whatever we needed to do to get to the financial point to make sure Blake was taken care of in case something happened to us.

We both chose to change!

We were highly motivated because our "why" had changed. We simply HAD to find a way to take care of Blake at the level we wanted. That was our "why" and we knew it would take hard work and determination, not to mention a real actionable plan.

So we took action, and a lot of it!

We researched what felt like a million ways to get to the place of financial security for Blake. There were two options that rose to the top that could help us hit our new sizeable financial goals; investing in real estate and building a successful business.

While we liked the idea of investing in real estate, it soon became evident that this approach would take too long to realize a significant return. Time we didn't feel we had for Blake's sake.

It became apparent that small business ownership was the way to go. We could build it, and when ready, sell it for a more sizable return on our investment.

While we were investigating entrepreneurship, God brought clarity for us on what we needed to do.

Blake's gymnastics accident received national media coverage, and subsequently a Dallas based massage therapist started following the updates on Blake's slow journey to recovery.

The massage therapist contacted Cindy at the Ronald McDonald House and shared with her that she specialized in providing therapeutic massage to individuals who suffered traumatic brain injuries, and thought her services would be helpful for Blake.

We agreed to give it a try alongside his current neuro-rehab and soon after we started noticing pronounced improvements with Blake's recovery.

Cindy called me one day to give me an update on Blake. As we chatted about the massage therapist and how she was making a difference in Blake's rehabilitation, something clicked for both of us. God had shown us what we should research for small business ownership.

There was only one issue with massage therapy ... neither of us knew a thing about it. All we knew was the impact it could have on people's lives.

So we started looking at franchise ownership with Massage Envy, the largest Massage franchise in the United States. We went through a due diligence process, and feeling it was the right thing to do, we signed our first franchise agreement and invested over $700,000 into our first location.

Quite a few people asked us, "Aren't you scared? You are investing a huge portion of what you have saved."

Our answer was, "Yes, but do you know what scares us more? It's what happens to Blake if something happens to us!" Cindy and I were committed to taking action toward achieving our goals and not letting emotion or F.E.A.R. (False Evidence Appearing Real) prevent us from doing so.

Initially we thought we would have two franchise locations in five years, but it went so well so quickly that we ended up with three franchise locations in just three years!

In addition to God's favor on our businesses, I believe the quick success we realized was due to the fact that we didn't have to try to figure everything out on our own: marketing, operations, recruiting, training, protocols, software systems, etc.

The franchisor had already proven out the model so all we needed to do was come in and implement everything as quickly and effectively as possible.

On the three-year anniversary of our businesses, I took Cindy to a steakhouse in Waco to celebrate. I asked her if she remembered the quote I read to her three years earlier about us doing what most would not do for just the next three years. She said, "yes".

Then I shared with her that in those three years we financially outperformed the previous 17 years combined!

We were both amazed that we had seen so much success in such a short amount of time.

I then asked, "Want to do it for three more years?"

"Absolutely," she replied.

Those three years were full of hard work and long hours, but they were also some of the best years of our lives.

So that night we celebrated two things. The first was the amazing progress we made toward hitting the life-plan goal for Blake that initially seemed insurmountable.

And secondly, I celebrated Cindy as the amazing businesswoman that she was as she didn't have this same confidence in herself prior to Blake's accident.

For personal reasons, Cindy was unable to finish her college degree. She is hard-working, smart and had consistently been promoted within the companies she worked for. However, time and time again she was told she couldn't advance within the company she worked for as she didn't have a college degree.

This happened one last time just prior to Blake's accident. Cindy was in the process of hiring employees that she would manage for more money than she was making, and when she asked her boss why, he said it was because they had a college degree, and she did not.

This really hurt Cindy and I saw her spirit shrivel. I felt their decision was incredibly short-sighted as at the time she was leading the department with the largest profit center in the company. I also shared with Cindy that her identity was not tied to a degree or what someone says about her, but who God says she is as His daughter. But it still hurt.

Fast forward after Blake's accident and starting the businesses, Cindy's spirit blossomed. She put the same skillset and work ethic that she used for others, and the only difference was that our family benefitted from all this hard work and not the companies she used to worked for.

This is what I would like to share with you in respect to reaching your own personal and financial goals. Wherever you are in your life journey today, it doesn't matter how old you are or how young you are, it doesn't matter how much money you have or how little money you have, it doesn't matter whether you have a degree or no degree, all that matters is this:

"If you will do what most will not do for just the next few years, then you can do what they cannot do for the rest of your life."

Will you?

We did exactly that, and we are so glad we did.

(And we still do it!)

– BOX #1 –

Dreams & Goals:

NEEDS:

Quality of Life:

– BOX #2 –

– Box #3 –

– Box #4 –

Chapter Three

Box #1 – Your Dreams and Goals

> "Whatever you vividly imagine, ardently desire, sincerely believe, and enthusiastically act upon … must inevitably come to pass!"
> – Paul J. Meyer

I heard in a seminar once that approximately 95% of the U.S. population "believed" that they would retire financially independent by age 65 without having to worry about government assistance. Do you know how many people they shared actually achieved this goal? Only 5%!

Now, I would bet that most people fully *intend* to, *plan* on, and *want* to retire with enough money in the bank to comfortably live on.

Not many actually *do*!

Sadly, that means over 95% of the US population is off track! Honestly evaluating their career path along the way would have been a good move, right?

Be honest:

> Are you part of that less than 5% ... or part of the over 95%?

Each of us must choose the path that will get us where we want to go.

Let's do a quick exercise together that should help you clearly define which rabbit you should be chasing at this time in your life. I will walk you through it now. It is also in the back of the book, so you can redo this as often as you like. (Feel free to scan it with your phone and send it to someone who needs it.)

You will also want to refer to this exercise later, so it's important that you complete it. Cindy and I refer to this exercise regularly as a way for us to reflect and to check on our forward progress.

Why? Because goals can change over time, new ones need to be added, and some need to be checked off the list once they have been accomplished.

I've seen this exercise help thousands of people get the clarity they have been looking for, and that clarity is vitally important because it is one of the secrets to hitting your dreams and goals.

Clarity! Do you have it?

The exercise is called the "4-Box Exercise." Before each of the subsequent chapters you will see a blank layout of the 4-Box Exercise that is gradually filled in.

At the start of this chapter is Box #1 and at the top of the box it says, "Dreams & Goals." In the middle it says, "Needs." At the bottom it says, "Quality of Life."

For a few minutes, I want you to think about some of your dreams and goals. But first I need you to do me a favor. This is not the time to be practical. I mean take the lid off! Dream BIG! There are no wrong answers. Where do you want to go, what do you want to have, and who do you want to become?

Do you want to own a lake home, a beach home, a mountain home? Do you want to travel the world? Do you want your own private jet with your own private pilot to fly you around? Remember, I said DREAM BIG!

One of Cindy's and my dreams and goals was to be able to travel the world and do as many fun, different things as we can and bring as many of our extended family along as possible at our expense (money often holds most families back from spending time with one another).

Many want to have their dream car (or dream cars) in their multi-car garage. Others want their dream home(s) in the ideal location(s) with the best views, weather, schools, nearby cities, family, amenities, vineyards, etc.

Some want to give to those in need, be philanthropic in and out of business, impact lives, and change the world. Others want to be a mayor, governor, senator, or even president of the United States.

Some want to travel commercially into outer space which is on Blake's and my list!

Take the lid off because dreams do not have to be practical.

If it can be vividly imagined, you know it's on someone's list!

Stop right here and make your list. Write down 20 dreams and goals that you have. Yes, it will take you a few minutes, but you owe it to yourself to make a list (random is fine) of 20 things you want to do, have, own, give away, share, etc.

But before doing so … if you are married or have a significant other, I highly encourage you to get with them at this point and work together on your dreams and goals list. Countless times, couples have shared with me how much they enjoyed dreaming together and getting on the same page.

After all, to achieve everything you want in life, it is imperative that you have the support of the one who loves and cares for you the most.

Now get to after it, take the lid off, and have fun!

1) _____
2) _____
3) _____
4) _____
5) _____
6) _____
7) _____
8) _____
9) _____
10) _____
11) _____
12) _____
13) _____
14) _____
15) _____
16) _____
17) _____
18) _____
19) _____
20) _____

These dreams and goals are your "wants." After these wants come the practical "needs" or necessary goals that you know you "have" to achieve.

Do you know what your needs are?

If you took the lid off to create your list of big dreams and goals, feel free to put the lid back on to accomplish this part. It's practical and very necessary.

What do you truly need?

That's a question people don't spend enough time thinking about. They really should, because when they accurately see their needs, they are less likely to be surprised by what's happening around them.

Here are a few sobering statistics that fluctuate year to year, but never seem to decrease monetarily:

- The average cost of a wedding is around $35,000.

- A single year of college in some schools can easily run over $50,000.

- Only 5% of the US population will be financially independent and able to retire without government assistance.

- Taking care of aging parents costs more every year.

- The cost of homes has doubled or tripled in many areas.

For someone to earn a passive income today of $50,000 to $60,000 a year, you need no less than one million dollars in the bank earning 5%-6% interest. With inflation and the cost of living going up, you could possibly need upwards of two to three times that amount 10 or 20 years from now. How much do you have in retirement today?

What's more, having a big income today doesn't necessarily translate into real wealth creation for tomorrow. My dad is a great example of that. At 74 years of age he called me out of the blue and asked if he could move in with us.

He had been a very successful realtor for more than 40 years, earning between $150,000 to over $300,000 per year. He drove a new Cadillac every other year and took all the vacations he wanted, but he had created no wealth with his money.

Cindy and I talked it over, prayed on it, and decided to move my dad in with us. The whole thing was very unexpected, but we had room in the house and we also knew it was our responsibility to care for our aging parents.

Unfortunately my dad also had health issues (he was on eight liters of oxygen a minute because he had COPD). He spent the last two years of his life with us and it was a blessing for everyone. I'm so glad we were able to do it!

My mother also worked hard most of her life as a banquet waitress. She didn't earn as much money, so she only received $1,100 a month from social security. I don't know where you can live in the U.S. today on only $1,100 a month!

My sister, niece, and our family have been blessed so that we have been able to help take care of my mom when and as needed. Do you and/or your spouse have parents who may need your financial help one day?

How about children? It isn't cheap raising children today. One day they will need a car, may go to college, and you may or may not want to financially support the wedding when they want to get married.

Your list of needs can also include potential needs. These are needs that may exist in the future, so you are preparing accordingly. Most people don't think enough about the future, much less prepare accordingly.

In truth, anyone who fails to prepare is ultimately preparing to fail.

That is why defining and knowing your needs is so very important. Blake's accident put this instantly in perspective for us.

Our dreams and goals hadn't changed, but our needs certainly did, and that fueled us to take action like never before.

As you did with your wants, take a few minutes to list some of your needs:

- _____
- _____
- _____
- _____
- _____
- _____
- _____
- _____
- _____
- _____
- _____
- _____
- _____

The last part of Box #1 is quality of life. Your quality of life is the direct result of you meeting the needs on your list.

You may want to read that again:

> Your quality of life is the direct result of you meeting the needs on your list.

For example, if one of your quality of life goals is to coach your child's sport team or to attend every game, then the corresponding need would be to figure out how to do that, how to afford it, what type of career or opportunity you will need to give you that time freedom, how much time you can take off from work, where you will live, etc.

I heard a story about a young man starting his dream job at a prestigious company. During his first week, the company had a retirement party for its highest producing salesperson.

They listed his career accomplishments and gave him a granite plaque and a gold watch in a wooden case. One of the audience members sitting next to the new hire leaned over and said, "Wow, that is an expensive watch!"

The young man, beaming with opportunity and wide eyes, asked, "Really, what is it? A Rolex?"

The audience member said, "No, that watch cost him three marriages and his relationship with his 27-year-old daughter who won't even talk to him."

Unfortunately, it's common for some people to confuse their career success with having a successful life. While a successful career can contribute to a successful life, there must be balance in all aspects of your life. I have been fortunate to have worked for a franchisor that focuses on helping both their franchisees and their associates to have balance in 6 areas of their lives.

Those 6 areas of life include:

1. Family
2. Career
3. Physical
4. Spiritual
5. Social
6. Mental

Think about quality of life. What does that mean to you? How many hours would you work? How often would you visit friends and family? Do you want to "become" happy and healthy? How much time would you like to devote to giving back? It's not all about how much we can make or take, but also how much we can give back to others in need of our time and resources.

As you did with your wants and needs, take a few minutes to list the important parts of the quality of life that you wish to have:

- _____
- _____
- _____
- _____
- _____
- _____
- _____
- _____

> "Be brave, little rabbit. Take a chance."
> – Cherise Sinclair

– BOX #1 –	– BOX #2 –
Dreams & Goals: • Beach Home • Travel the World • Ferrari • Outer Space **NEEDS:** • Retirement • Kid's College • Care of Parents • Wedding(s) **Quality of Life:** • Less Stress • More Vacation • No Work Travel • Giving Back	If things continue over the next 3+ years as they have over the past 3 years, and you make no significant changes, will you be on track to accomplish your Dreams, Goals, Needs, and Quality of Life Requirements? **Circle:** **YES** – or – **NO**

– Box #3 –

– Box #4 –

Chapter Four

Box #2 –
The Fork in the Road

> "The man who chases two rabbits,
> catches neither."
> – Confucius

Hopefully at this point you have written down many of your dreams and goals, made your list of the needs necessary to achieve your wants, and defined the quality of life requirements you want.

I ask that you consider again this question:

> If things continue over the next 3+ years as they have over the last 3 years, without making any real significant changes, will you be on track to accomplishing all your dreams and goals, needs, and quality of life requirements?

It's a YES/NO question. Which is it for you?

Yes ___ or No ___

If your answer is "Yes," then keep doing what you are doing! Good job. Keep at it. Drive faster and be sure to check in from time to time to make sure you are still on track!

If your answer is "No," then you have one of two choices to make:

1. Change – do something about it

   or

2. Give up – stop chasing your dream or goal

What do most people do? Statistically we saw earlier that most people (over 9 out of 10) will give up on their dreams and goals. I believe the biggest reason for them not doing what is needed is because they never had the opportunity that you just had in clearly defining your dreams and goals, needs, and quality of life requirements.

Sure, most people "hope" that someday things will turn out differently, but they are basically just burying their heads in the sand. Please hear me when I say, "hope" is not a strategy to bet your and your family's financial and quality of future life on.

Most close their eyes and hope that with a little luck and fairy dust, maybe they will arrive somewhere … somewhere that they didn't know where it was, how they were to get there, or what it would look like when they got there!

Sounds like a magical place! And for all but a lucky few, it's not going to happen.

Sadly, one day they will have the taste of regret and say, "I wish …"

- "I would've"
- "I could've"
- "I should've"

But it's too late.

When Cindy and I tasted our reality, that we were not on track to be financially independent, together we admitted our reality. We acknowledged the need to change course. And we took action.

We were not going to give up. We are all Blake had and he depended on us!

What about you? If you answered no, are your dreams and goals, needs, quality of life requirements for you and loved ones worth fighting for?

So, if your answer was "no," what will you do?

During my years of coaching, it has been my observation that most people looking to start a business never stop to take the time to fully understand why they are doing so. For those who don't take the time, they usually end up finding reasons not to do so.

Lack of clarity on why you are starting a business will typically lead to the wrong decisions because they are based more on emotions and not the facts. Would you agree with me that the best decisions are based on facts and not emotions?

If you truly took the time up to this point to determine why you are needing to start a business (dreams & goals, needs, quality of life requirements), you now have the foundation to determine what business vehicle is best for you to achieve those goals.

This is by far the biggest decision you needed to make in this whole process, and that is: I need to do something different (in this case start a business) to help me achieve my goals, and I am willing to do what it takes to achieve my goals.

I will not give up like the other 95% that do.

If you see that change is required so that you can reach your dreams and goals, do you know what those changes are?

It is admittedly a harsh revelation to recognize that the path you are currently on may not actually get you to your goals.

That hurts, but isn't it better to adjust now while you can than keep going and pay for it later?

I like how Denzel Washington says it:

> "Do what you gotta do so you can do what you wanna do."

If you are anything like Cindy and me, giving up on your dreams and goals is not something you are willing to do.

And after completing the earlier goals exercise, you now have a very clear idea of the lifestyle you want that comes with your dreams and goals.

I can tell you countless stories of people who came to this realization and made the necessary changes. They ended up hitting their dreams and goals because of it.

Pressing on, refusing to give up, and welcoming change are much easier when you have a compelling and motivating "why" behind you.

Cindy and I knew our "why." It was the unknown of what would happen to Blake if something happened to us. Who would take care of him?

Knowing our "why" led us to change.

In all honesty, we had to change. It was crucial or we would never have been on track to hit our dreams and goals and to take care of our son.

We were willing to endure any "how" because we knew our "why."

No, we didn't know everything. We didn't know the exact steps. We took risks. We stretched. We worked hard.

Likewise, you don't have to know everything that is to come next. You don't have to see, touch, or understand every aspect of your required change right now.

All you need to do at this precise moment is to accept that change is required and commit to making those changes.

With that, you have taken the first step. After you acknowledge that change is required, you can build.

Let me ask you a question before moving onto the next chapter, Box #3. If you are married or have a significant other, are you both on the same page as to whether your answer to Box #2 is YES or NO?

From my experience, most couples end up with the same answer, but that's not always the case. Sometimes one person may believe they need to make the necessary changes to accomplish their goals, while the other believes they are already on track.

I have had couples go back and forth in front of me expressing their reasoning to one another. Most of the time it comes down to one of these three reasons:

1. One person's lack of understanding of their true financial position.

2. One person's goals are more aspirational than the others.

3. One person is fearful in taking the step towards business ownership.

Were Cindy and I fearful in taking our step towards business ownership? Yes! Please know that this emotion is normal, and most people experience it when making a big decision like starting a business.

However, the reason you are working through this 4-Box exercise is to help you determine what is most important for you and your family, and not let an *emotion* prevent you from doing what is necessary to achieve your family's goals.

Most successful businesses that I've seen tend to have one thing in common; the business owners, in this case a couple, are in full agreement in starting and building a business.

This doesn't mean that they both need to be involved in the day-to-day building of the business, as the one may be a stay-at-home parent or have a career of their own. But having this collective support of one another is essential as some days are tougher than others.

Prior to Blake's accident, Cindy and I would always ask how our days were at work. Some days we would celebrate the wins, but some days it was important to be a sounding board when things didn't go so well.

This doesn't change when you start a business and why it's important to be aligned with your decision before moving forward together.

So, if you are currently still undecided as a couple, then I encourage you to take the time to have an open and constructive dialogue so you both can work towards either a collective YES or NO.

After doing so, if your collective answer is a YES and are currently on track to accomplish all your dreams, goals, needs, and quality of life requirements from Box #1, then keep doing what you are doing as mentioned earlier.

If it's a collective NO and not currently on track, now is the time to move on to the next chapter.

– Box #1 –

Dreams & Goals:

- Beach Home
- Travel the World
- Ferrari
- Outer Space

NEEDS:

- Retirement
- Kid's College
- Care of Parents
- Wedding(s)

Quality of Life:

- Less Stress
- More Vacation
- No Work Travel
- Giving Back

– Box #2 –

If things continue over the next 3+ years as they have over the past 3 years, and you make no significant changes, will you be on track to accomplish your Dreams, Goals, Needs, and Quality of Life Requirements?

Circle:

YES – or – **(NO)**

– Box #3 –

What kind of business?

What size of business?

How does the business need to be structured?

– Box #4 –

CHAPTER FIVE

Box #3 – The "How" to Your "Why"

"When you know your why, you can endure any how." – John O'Leary

Over the years, I have had the opportunity to help so many people through this very process of seeing that change is needed and then taking the necessary next steps to move forward.

Along the way, I looked for clues for common success factors, and have found two factors that are most common in those who change course and achieve their dreams and goals.

Here they are:

> **Common Factor #1:** For most people, their dreams and goals are only achievable if they build something they own that can generate the kind of income necessary to fund what they really want.

Common Factor #2: For most people, the income they earn from their day-to-day jobs is not sufficient or sustainable to really fund their dreams and goals.

And that leads right into Box #3, the "how" part of the equation. You know your "why."

Now comes the "how" part.

Most likely, acknowledging the need for change is more of a confirmation than anything else.

Maybe you've sensed it, wondered, or toyed with the idea, but it has not caught you entirely unaware.

Perhaps your thinking goes like this:

1. I see that change is required to reach my dreams and goals.

    and

2. I understand that my current path isn't going to get me where I want to go, if at all or not quickly enough.

So what's next? That is the real question.

Have you thought about owning your own business? Have you wondered if owning your own business would be necessary to reach your dreams and goals?

Most people facing the urgency of change will wonder that same thing.

Here is a fact worth considering very carefully:

> Most people who make the necessary changes to achieve their dreams and goals do so by owning their own business.

When you build your own business, you are creating equity that will directly benefit you and your family. Equity ownership in a business is valuable and creates options for you later on.

You will be able to sell it one day when you are ready to capture that equity. Likewise, you could have a succession plan and pass it on.

And controlling your income is always better than someone else controlling it for you, right? And you'll never worry again about being "just a number" or being laid off.

You might be thinking, "Okay, that's a good thought, but what type of business would that be?"

That's why we are here.

At the top of the box #3 it asks, "What kind of business?"

In the middle it asks, "What size of business?"

And at the bottom it asks, "How does it need to be structured?"

It is imperative that you answer these questions. They are the seeds of your blueprint to success.

For example, when thinking of what kind of business you should start, you have many options. Are you thinking of starting a landscaping business? A plumbing business? An essential business? A restaurant business? Maybe you have some sort of passion or calling to a particular industry or niche.

Blake's accident put the massage industry on our radar. Neither Cindy nor I had any experience in the massage world, but it "clicked" for us when we saw the value and benefit for others.

We knew we wanted to help people. That was important to us, but there are countless product and service opportunities out there. Which to choose from?

Cindy and I talked a lot about our interests, skills, likes, dislikes, etc. And while we liked the idea of helping people (with massage therapy) the way our son had been helped, what was MORE important to us was that the business we built be able to help us achieve our goals, which included putting Blake in a place of financial security.

There are so many options out there. The choice is yours. Don't get trapped in thinking (or listening to negative voices) that says you must first be an expert in an industry before you can start your own business.

Remember, my wife and I had never even given a massage before we jumped into the massage industry.

Next, determining the size of business (in terms of dollars, revenue, profit) that is needed is essential as it must provide you the amount of money you need to accomplish your dreams, goals, needs, and quality of life requirements.

The bigger your goals, the bigger your business will need to be. Please know that the first business you start may not be the last. For many the first business is the vehicle to help generate enough profit to fund additional businesses or investments.

The key here is to focus on getting the first business up and running and profitable so you can then reinvest in other future businesses.

The structure of the business answers the question of whether the business is built around you or someone else. Are you the person doing the work or are you the person managing others who are doing the work? Do you have systems and processes in place so you can take family vacations and not have to worry about your business struggling when you are gone?

So many questions, but they are all good and necessary for you to answer at this point in your journey.

For most people who are facing change, these are their three choices or questions:

1. Do you build something from scratch that is unproven and/or that you have limited experience in?

2. Do you explore buying someone else's business?

3. Do you invest in a franchise that is established with systems, marketing, coaching, technology, and support?

Before you jump in, whether starting your own business, buying a business, or starting a franchise business, consider the position that you desire to have within the business.

Some people leave corporate America to work for themselves, only to find themselves in another "job." They become the key cog in the wheel and have no freedom of time. Or will your business provide you with the freedom of time and wealth to fund and fuel your dreams and goals, needs, and quality of life requirements you have identified?

That's clearly a loaded question (on purpose), so think it through. Plan it out. Don't jump until you know for sure (to the best of your ability) that you are going in the right direction.

Box #3 is designed to help you determine which business vehicle is best for you.

Naturally, everyone is different, but I have found a lot of people like the franchise ownership option because they get help and get started right away with a needed product or service that has proven systems. "Proven" means someone has hired the experts, spent the time, and spent the money to find out what works and what doesn't work.

Quite simply, the fact that it is proven increases the odds of your success considerably!

Because Cindy and I knew nothing about the massage industry, much less running our own massage business, we spent our time finding a company with systems where they had those pieces already figured out.

I saw the company, Massage Envy, and their franchise opportunity as a vehicle to help get us to our dreams and goals.

We knew we would have to do the work ("drive the vehicle," so to speak), but we also knew we didn't want (nor did we have the skill set) to spend our time creating a business from scratch.

I know me ... I love my cars. I love to drive. I feel connected with the experience. But I am no car builder!

We knew our family would be better served by finding an existing vehicle that we could jump right into and follow the road that had already been proven to take people where they wanted to go.

Also, I was no stranger to seeing the success that franchise owners enjoyed. I had worked in and around franchising for decades.

I have seen thousands of entrepreneurs take a step into business ownership with proven systems. I always admired their courage to start a franchise and their drive (their motivating "why" behind it all) to jump into business ownership.

It only made sense for us to do the same. I had personally seen the track record, and it was thousands strong. We also knew that the final decision wasn't up to us. We thought we would be great fits for Massage Envy and their culture, but franchises are *awarded*, not *bought*.

There is a mutual evaluation process that prospective owners and franchisors go through that brings clarity to everyone involved. The evaluation process includes a lot of questions, digging, and due diligence as being awarded a franchise is not only a big decision for you and your family, but also for the franchisor. It is a marriage of sorts, with a common goal of successful small business ownership.

While you are doing your research to determine if the franchise brand you are considering is successful, know that they will most likely be doing the same with you.

The best franchisors try to find individuals who have been successful in their past. As when they are surrounded with business coaches and mentors, marketing and support, training and technology … they don't become less successful, but more successful!

So, if you have had success in the past, why would your level of success be any different when you start with a proven successful business model?

Experience and statistics show this formula to be consistently true and accurate:

>A successful system with support
>+
>a successful person
>=
>a greater level of success on both sides

Most importantly, following a proven system is the path to obtain your dreams and goals.

Cindy, with absolutely no massage experience, built her Massage Envy locations to the #1 spot in the system of over 1,100 locations!

For you, it doesn't matter what your background might be or how much or how little money you have. All that matters is knowing "why" you are doing what you are doing.

When you know your "why," all you need is the "how," and when you find that, you are off to the races!

Okay, so how do you know how to find the right franchise opportunity? That's a fair question to ask, and you should be asking it.

Early in my years in franchising, one of my mentors, Mike Hawkins, would often ask people considering starting their own business this question: "Do you currently have a written criteria to evaluate franchise opportunities, so when you find the right one, you know it's the right one?"

The answer most often was, "No."

Mike would then work with the individual to make a list of what was most important for them in starting a business. This provided the candidate with a good benchmark to compare different opportunities.

Cindy and I took Mike's advice, and over the years we have created our own list of criteria when looking for with franchise opportunities.

One criteria item high on our list is finding a business that can be run by someone other than us. I'm not saying we wouldn't be involved in the business, but the success of the business wouldn't be dependent upon us being involved in the day-to-day. We see this as imperative as it relates to our exit strategy.

If you asked most small business owners if they could take their family on a vacation for three to six months, what do you think they say their business would look like when they returned home? I've asked this question to many myself, and most of them say it would be in shambles, disarray, and some even say it wouldn't be open when they returned home.

This is difficult to hear as most people starting a small business do it so that they can have a nest egg one day when they go to sell it. Let me ask you this, how much would you pay for a business that would be in shambles, disarray or even closed if the business owner left for an extended period of time? If you're anything like me, I wouldn't buy it, and if I did, it wouldn't be for much!

Now let's say a different owner came back from their extended vacation and their business was not only doing well, but continued to grow when they were gone? Do you think that business would be much more appealing to buyers? Absolutely!

When Cindy and I are considering different franchise opportunities, we start with the end in mind. We focus on ones that have proven systems, processes, clear organizational charts, and a history of successful sales from previous owners.

Why is this? Because we want to receive the highest multiple of EBITDA (earnings before interest, taxes, depreciation, and amortization) when we go to sell our business one day. A healthy EBITDA allows a buyer to pay more as the business generates enough cash profit to pay their debt service, reinvest in the business for growth, and pay them a salary or dividends.

If "we are the business," there would be little or no cash profits beyond what we would pay ourselves, and this is not appealing to most buyers. The only reason we were able to sell our businesses for the multiple of EBITDA that we did was not only because they were very profitable, but because we "worked on" the businesses, and "not in" the businesses.

There are two other high priority criteria that are important to us; recurring services and having the ability to scale with other locations. We like having business models that have recurring services to the same customer since we believe it provides:

1. Higher margins over time as we don't have to pay to acquire the customer again.

2. More value to a future buyer as they are receiving active customers and therefore cashflow from day one.

We also prefer working with franchisors that will provide us the ability to expand by acquiring additional locations or diversifying with any available sister brands. This allows us to scale our growth and, in some cases, leverage our existing customers by providing them additional services.

The following is a 20-point checklist that has helped Cindy and I discern which franchise opportunity matched our requirements the best.

While it would be rare for one business to match all 20-points on any list of criteria, we did make sure the business we chose matched the most important criteria for us.

Criteria to Evaluate a Franchise

1. Can the business be run by someone other than us?

2. Does the business model have recurring customers?

3. Can we acquire additional franchises within the same franchise system?

4. Is the business model recession resistant? (No business is recession proof, but there certainly are companies that are recession resistant.)

5. Does the company have established and well-known brands?

6. Does the company have proven systems built into these 10 areas: Pricing, Marketing, Sales Systems, Finance and Benchmarking, Statistical Tracking, Management Training so someone can run your business for you one day, Recruiting Solutions, On-Going Business Owner Training, Frontline Customer Service Systems and Human Resource Solutions?

7. What kind of training does the franchise offer after the initial start-up training? Do they have regional training meetings, financial training, field training, monthly webinars, or training at their annual reunion or conference?

8. What kind of coaching do they provide? (Marketing Coach, Business Coach, Technical Training Coach, Technology Software Coach)

9. What kind of quality of life does the business offer? Is it M-F, nights, weekends, or 24/7 every day of the week?

10. What kind of vendors do they have to help cut costs?

11. Do they encourage you to visit their home office? If so, do they require you to bring a check and expect you to sign a contract before you leave?

12. Does the franchisor compete for business with their franchisees?

13. Does the franchisor provide cross-marketing opportunities with their other brands within their franchise system?

14. What type of resale department do they have?

15. Do we have a protected territory?

16. What kind of networking opportunities will we have with the other franchisees in the franchise system?

17. Are they concerned about us personally so we can achieve our personal and financial goals? Do they teach goal setting to help keep our lives balanced?

18. What kind of research and development do they do?

19. How dedicated is the franchisor with social media and digital marketing?

20. Do they have a code of ethics and values that they make decisions by?

In the back of this book, you have an opportunity to create your own criteria list that is important to you when looking for the right franchise opportunity.

Feel free to use any on Cindy's and my list above, and to take off any criteria that aren't as important to you and add others that should be on your list.

At the end of the day, this is about you finding the right opportunity that meets your personal criteria so you can accomplish your personal and financial goals.

"Opportunity comes like a snail, and once it has passed you, it changes into a fleet rabbit and is gone."
– Arthur Brisbane

– Box #1 –

Dreams & Goals:

- Beach Home
- Travel the World
- Ferrari
- Outer Space

NEEDS:

- Retirement
- Kid's College
- Care of Parents
- Wedding(s)

Quality of Life:

- Less Stress
- More Vacation
- No Work Travel
- Giving Back

– Box #2 –

If things continue over the next 3+ years as they have over the past 3 years, and you make no significant changes, will you be on track to accomplish your Dreams, Goals, Needs, and Quality of Life Requirements?

Circle:

YES – or – (NO)

– Box #3 –	– Box #4 –
What kind of business? • Home Services • Restaurant • Retail Services • Vacation Travel **What size of business?** • Income & Profits needed to achieve goals **How does the business need to be structured?** • Your role in the business • Systems/Process	**Consequences** **Victims**

Chapter Six

Box #4 – The Mirror

> "When you realize the man staring back at you in the mirror is both your PROBLEM and your SOLUTION, your whole world will change."
> – Calvin B. Peterson

Have you ever wondered what would happen if you did NOT reach your intended target? I mean, what would happen if you failed to achieve your dreams and goals?

Stated more boldly; if you never accomplish your dreams, goals, needs, and quality of life requirements, what would be the consequences of that, and who would be the victims of those consequences besides yourself?

This challenging question highlights that the decisions we make, whether to do something or do nothing, will not only impact us, but so many others around us.

In most cases it impacts the ones we love the most including our spouse/significant other, our children, our parents, our church, our community and so many others.

I'm not trying to be negative or doom and gloom. Not at all! Rather, it's the exact opposite.

My sincere hope is to help you accomplish your dreams and goals, needs, and quality of life requirements. (That is, after all, the whole plan and purpose for this book!)

But sometimes it helps to consider the "worst case" scenario. It gives perspective as well as incentive.

The fourth and final box does just that. It holds up a mirror to your life and helps you understand why you are doing what you must do to accomplish your dreams and goals.

The whole point of this is to make the necessary changes now, while you still can, rather than waiting and inevitably living a life of regret. That's not an option either!

So, what are some of the outcomes in your life if you do not make a change now?

For us, the consequence of not hitting our dreams and goals was obvious. Blake depended on us in every way.

We absolutely HAD to create $12-$23 million, according to the life plan company, just for our son to be taken care of, much less for us to show him and the rest of our family the full life that is possible when dreams and goals are attained.

For us, failing to hit our dreams and goals meant:

- Inability to care for Blake long-term
- Blake going to a state-run facility for the rest of his life in the event something happened to us
- My mom not living comfortably in her golden years
- Not able to provide a legacy to our grandchildren
- Lack of freedom to do what we want when we want both now and in the future
- Opportunities lost by not being able to afford to do what we know is good and right
- Not able to bless our church, community, friends, and family financially to the extent God has provided us opportunity to do so
- We wouldn't be able to help our employees accomplish their personal and financial goals

There are many other consequences, but you get the idea.

Now, take a moment on the next page to write down some of the consequences of not hitting your dreams and goals, meeting all of your needs, and attaining the quality of life that you want:

- _____
- _____
- _____
- _____
- _____
- _____
- _____
- _____
- _____
- _____
- _____
- _____
- _____
- _____
- _____
- _____
- _____
- _____
- _____
- _____
- _____
- _____
- _____
- _____
- _____
- _____

If you don't achieve your dreams and goals, what would your answers be to these questions:

Will you be able to travel to where you've always dreamed of going?
Yes/No _____

Will you be able to eat healthy foods of your choice?
Yes/No _____

Will you be able to drive the car(s) that you want?
Yes/No _____

Will you be able to live where you want?
Yes/No _____

Will you be able to be an active participant in your children's and/or grandchildren's lives?
Yes/No _____

Will you be able to pay for college for your children or grandchildren?
Yes/No _____

Will you be able to retire when you planned and enjoy your retirement to the fullest?
Yes/No _____

Will you be able to create and live the legacy that you want to leave behind?
Yes/No _____

Ask yourself tough questions now, because now is the best time to find those answers!

At the top of box #4 it says, "Consequences."

In the middle it says, "Victims."

If you fail to accomplish your dreams and goals, needs, and quality of life requirements, there truly would be consequences, wouldn't there?

I know "consequences" may sound like a harsh word, but that is intentional. It is there because when we know we should do something and we don't, that choice not to act has consequences.

And those who would be impacted by those consequences would be, in a sense, the victims. Isn't that true?

There really would be "victims" if you fail to achieve your dreams and goals. I'm simply calling it what it is as we look in the mirror.

For us, Blake would be the biggest victim if we failed to meet our dreams and goals. We would also be the victims, as would our entire family and network of friends.

Another way to think of victims is to ask yourself this question:

Who, besides myself, will be affected the most if I do not accomplish my dreams, goals, needs, and quality of life requirements? Make a list below:

- _____
- _____
- _____
- _____
- _____
- _____
- _____
- _____
- _____
- _____
- _____
- _____
- _____
- _____
- _____
- _____
- _____

If you are anything like Cindy and me, this part of the exercise can hit hard. Being vulnerable and honest with our answers allows us to look at the impact of our decisions with eyes wide open and provides us the clarity and the resolve to do what is needed.

It's better to face these realities now than to be forced to do so later when you are older and may not have the time, health, or resources.

Time is truly of the essence. You are worth it and so are the ones who are counting on you.

Failure was not an option for us. While we walked Blake through his road to full restoration, the consequences of us not hitting our dreams and goals were always apparent. There would have been many victims and sad consequences, with Blake being the first on every list, but we chose to never let that happen.

Whatever your dreams and goals might be, I challenge you ... don't let anything get between you and your dreams, goals, needs, and quality of life requirements.

Absolutely nothing!

– Box #1 –

Dreams & Goals:

- Beach Home
- Travel the World
- Ferrari
- Outer Space

NEEDS:

- Retirement
- Kid's College
- Care of Parents
- Wedding(s)

Quality of Life:

- Less Stress
- More Vacation
- No Work Travel
- Giving Back

– Box #2 –

If things continue over the next 3+ years as they have over the past 3 years, and you make no significant changes, will you be on track to accomplish your Dreams, Goals, Needs, and Quality of Life Requirements?

Circle:

YES – *or* – **(NO)**

– Box #3 –

What kind of business?

- Home Services
- Restaurant
- Retail Services
- Vacation Travel

What size of business?

- Income & Profits needed to achieve goals

How does the business need to be structured?

- Your role in the business
- Systems/Process

– Box #4 –

Consequences

- I will have to work into retirement
- Not be able to travel and go on dream vacations

Victims

- My Children
- My Spouse
- My Parents
- My Church

Chapter Seven

Your Definition

"The definition of success is getting many of the things money can buy and all the things money can't buy." – Zig Ziglar

Now that you have completed the 4-Box exercise and understand both the depth and importance of achieving your goals, it is time to create your own personal definition of financial independence.

Think about what you want YOUR end goal to look like, and then memorialize it below. Feel free to use parts of our definition if it aligns with what you are wanting to accomplish.

Either way I recommend that you make it specific, concise, and readily accessible.

Whether you tape it on your bathroom mirror or keep it as your screensaver on your phone, referring to this definition will help you determine if the decisions you are making daily are taking you towards or away from your goals.

As a reminder, here is the definition that Robert helped Cindy and me create:

> By the age of 55, we will have a minimum of $5,000,000 of income-producing assets generating a minimum of 5% return, which will provide $250,000 a year of passive income without working and no real personal debt.

Now take some time to fill out your personal definition below:

By the age of _____, I/we will have:

_____
_____
_____
_____
_____
_____
_____
_____
_____
_____
_____
_____
_____
_____
_____
_____
_____

Again, I encourage you to put your personal definition in a visible place so that you see it every single day.

Over time it will not only become easy for you to recite your definition from memory, but also notice that the decisions you make on a daily basis will start taking you towards the goals and not away from them.

> "The wise bunny knows the carrot will not hop to him."
> – Krista Lester

Conclusion

Always Adjust

"Everyone has a plan until they get punched in the face." – Mike Tyson

When NASA sent the men to the moon in 1969, the spaceship was off course most of the time. They simply made constant small adjustments along the way.

Adjustments are good and necessary. Anytime you aren't sure of your next step, it's probably time to make a small adjustment.

It's all good! There is nothing wrong with adjustments.

In truth, we are all works in progress. Nobody is perfect. And that means we can and should continually tweak and adjust our plans so that we hit our intended targets.

Unfortunately, most people think that making an adjustment is a sign of failure. But it's not! To adjust means you are smart, aware, and proactive.

It also means you are more likely to achieve your dreams and goals!

Regularly take time to evaluate your choices. In fact, I recommend that you read through this book every few years. Challenge yourself to be precisely on target.

Success is always going to come to those who know where they are going and keep at it. That means always adjusting.

You are a work in progress. We all are. So be proud of it, make those necessary tweaks and adjustments, and keep on chasing your dreams and goals.

It's your life we are talking about, so it's clearly worth it!

Years back, when I honestly evaluated my progress toward financial independence with Robert Tunmire, we were only halfway to my goal.

Then Blake had his accident.

And suddenly we were WAY short of our goal of financial independence.

If there was ever time to adjust, it was then. We flat out knew we could not hit our target if we stayed on our current path. We simply had to do something different, very different!

We worked through the 4-Box plan, just as you have seen here. And we made the necessary changes that also changed the trajectory of our family.

The required $12-$23 million to take care of Blake seemed utterly impossible, but when you believe, the impossible becomes possible.

We grew our massage franchise, expanded to multiple locations, and eventually were courted by private equity firms interested in acquiring what we had created.

We evaluated their offers, and ultimately ended up selling our successful business.

Our impossible became our reality!

Blake will never have to go to a state institution because Cindy and I put a stake in the ground and chose to chase our dreams and goals with passion and vigor.

When we sold our massage business, Cindy leaned toward me and said, "Are you ready to do it again?" Initially I said something of the sort, "Are you crazy?! We just spent 6 years building these businesses, sold them for more than we could had ever imagined, and now you want to do it again?

She said she already missed building her businesses, and even more missed helping so many of her employees accomplish their own personal goals along the way. She was right.

We had developed some amazing relationships with our team members to the extent that some of them followed us to our next adventure of opening 6 more franchises.

So, our dreams and goals have continued to grow through our journey, and so has Blake's story. When he graduated from Texas Tech University with honors, he *walked* across the stage to receive his diploma! There are no words that can express the joy and emotions that Cindy and I, and so many others, experienced that day.

Today Blake works at a local coffee shop in Waco and has started sharing his story as a public speaker at events and conferences nationwide. Blake's recovery story starting in the hospital was captured by a film crew for over 5+ years and you can see his journey (and how we determined to start our businesses) by visiting **www.HiImBlake.com** (Hi I'm Blake).

Our God is a God of healing, and our son did walk out of that hospital, and he continues to walk in pursuit of his own dreams and goals!

I know you can do the same!

– Box #1 –	– Box #2 –
Dreams & Goals: • • • • **NEEDS:** • • • • **Quality of Life:** • • • •	If things continue over the next 3+ years as they have over the past 3 years, and you make no significant changes, will you be on track to accomplish your Dreams, Goals, Needs, and Quality of Life Requirements? **Circle:** **YES** – *or* – **NO**

– Box #3 –

What kind of business?

-
-
-

What size of business?

-
-
-
-

How does the business need to be structured?

-
-
-
-

– Box #4 –

Consequences

-
-
-
-
-
-

Victims

-
-
-
-
-

> "Everything that is real was imagined first."
> – The Velveteen Rabbit, by Margery Williams

Franchise Criteria

-
-
-
-
-

Franchise Criteria

-

-

-

-

-

Franchise Criteria

-
-
-
-
-

Notes to Self

Notes to Self

"To 'pull a rabbit out of a hat' means achieving something remarkable, surprising, or solving a problem through unexpected means."
– U.S. Dictionary (usdictionary.com)

About the Author

Pat Hyland has worked in and around franchising for over 30 years. He received his Certified Franchise Executive designation in 2014 from the International Franchise Association. With a servant-hearted mindset, Pat helps aspiring entrepreneurs determine if business ownership is right for them, and if so, he helps them determine which opportunity would be best for them. He has been in executive leadership in franchising for both a franchisor and as a franchisee. He has trained over 2,500 small business owners in marketing their services to consumers, recruiting top talent, and goal setting. One of Pat's passions is to train franchise development professionals and help them become the best in their field. Together, Pat and his wife Cindy are Multi-Unit, Multi-Concept franchise owners and believe strongly in the franchise sector.

www.StopChasingTwoRabbits.com